"What an invaluable book! Thomas Hardy's vivid, surprising, and metrically resourceful elegies, so ruthlessly truthful and wrenchingly clear, so filled with nostalgia and remorse, so tender, grief-stricken, and alive, are one of the great, shattering, open-hearted legacies of twentieth-century English poetry. We are made more human in reading them."   —EDWARD HIRSCH

"A superb volume of forty poignant lyrics by one of the half-dozen major poets of the English language in the twentieth century."
—HAROLD BLOOM

"Thomas Hardy's strange and beautiful elegies for his wife are among the most human and moving masterpieces of modern poetry. They mark the moment when this great novelist— already in his early sixties—becomes one the great poets of the English language. Alternately tortured and tender, the poems delve as deeply into the contradictions of the human heart as Hardy's finest novels."   —DANA GIOIA

"Perhaps the strangest suite of love elegies in the language, Hardy's 'Poems of 1912–1913' mix passion, memory, love, remorse, regret, self-awareness and self-flagellation into an incomparable lyric brew, bringing originally inflected traditional meters (ballad, narrative, song) to serve a speech of intense emotional immediacy and candor, all in celebration of his dead (and for many years estranged) wife, Emma. Often lost in the abundance of Hardy's larger collections, these poems about Emma deserve their own space, a space worthy of their 'radiant vitality' and 'salt-edged,' scarifying honesty. In this little jewel-box of a book they have found it."   —EAMON GRENNAN

The church at St. Juliot, near Boscastle.
WATERCOLOR, COURTESY OF THE ARTIST, GEORGE WICKHAM.

Unexpected Elegies
Thomas Hardy

"Poems of 1912–13"
and Other Poems About Emma

Selected, with an introduction by
Claire Tomalin

A Karen and Michael Braziller Book
Persea Books / New York

The publisher wishes to thank the Dorset County Museum,
Dorchester, England, for its invaluable cooperation in the assembling
of this volume, especially in allowing the use of photographs
from its archives and paintings by George Wickham.

Copyright © 2010 by Persea Books, Inc.
Introduction copyright © 2010 by Claire Tomalin

All rights reserved. No part of this publication may be reproduced or transmitted
in any form or by any means, electronic or mechanical, including photocopy,
recording, or any information storage and retrieval system without prior permis-
sion in writing from the publisher.

To request permission to reprint or to make copies, and/or for any other informa-
tion, please write to the publisher:

Persea Books, Inc.
853 Broadway
New York, NY 10003

Library of Congress Cataloging-in-Publication Data
Hardy, Thomas, 1840–1928.
Unexpected elegies : Poems of 1912–13, and other poems about Emma/Thomas
Hardy; selected, with an introduction by Claire Tomalin.—1st ed.
     p. cm.
"A Karen and Michael Braziller book."
Includes bibliographical references.
ISBN: 978-0-89255-361-7 (alk. paper)
1. Hardy, Emma Lavinia Gifford, 1840–1912—Poetry. 2. Hardy, Emma Lavinia
Gifford, 1840–1912—Death—Poetry. 3. Authors' spouses—England—Poetry.
4. Loss (Psychology)—Poetry. 5. Elegiac poetry, English. I. Tomalin, Claire.
II. Hardy, Thomas, 1840–1928. Poems of 1912–13. III. Title.
PR4741.T66 2010
821'.8—dc22
                              2010015397

Designed by Rita Lascaro
Typeset in Goudy Old Style and Avenir
Manufactured in the United States of America
First Edition

CONTENTS

POEMS OF 1912–13

OTHER POEMS ABOUT EMMA

*The publisher wishes to acknowledge and to thank
Helen Handley Houghton
for her invaluable editorial work
on all aspects of this book.*

DURING THE 1890s, Thomas Hardy wrote what may be his least known novel, *The Well-Beloved*, published in 1897, which tells the life story of a sculptor whose temperament allows him to fall in love repeatedly but never to remain in love with any one woman for long. The book pleased and interested Marcel Proust, who saw in it a mirror of his own idea, that the lover creates an image of the beloved in his mind and attaches it to someone whom it may not fit at all. In Hardy's tale each young woman seems to embody the sculptor's ideal, full of "radiant vitality," until the glory departs from her and she becomes to him in his own words, "a corpse." Another young woman succeeds her, becoming his ideal until she too fades and is rejected; and then another. Sensibly, the sculptor never marries. One day in old age, he is looking through an album of photographs and lights on an image of an early love who he now believes to be dead. Suddenly, "he loved the woman dead and inaccessible as he had never loved her in life . . . the times of youthful friendship with her, in which he had learnt every note of her innocent nature, flamed up into a yearning and passionate attachment, embittered by regret beyond words."

The passage reads almost like a prophecy of what happened to Hardy after the death of his first wife, Emma, in 1912, when he found himself enthrall to her as he had not been for decades. But the real Hardy's reaction makes for a much more riveting tale than the one contained in his 1897 novel. Hardy transformed his hopelessly revived love into poetry; the poems he conjured up as he mourned the death of his wife and celebrated the love they had once shared must be the most unexpected elegies ever written. The long history of how they came about is full of surprises and still has the power to shock. And although poems must stand alone by their own strength, and these do, this is one of the occasions when biography is able to throw light on their genesis and significance and add to our appreciation of them.

Thomas Hardy and Emma Gifford met in 1870, when both were approaching thirty. They fell in love and, facing off the opposition of both their families, married in 1874. Emma's people, the Giffords, were against the marriage on the grounds of class difference. Her father, even though he was an almost penniless drunkard who had abandoned his profession of solicitor, could not countenance his middle-class daughter, brought up as a lady, marrying the son of a poor country builder. Hardy's mother, who was opposed to the idea of marriage in general, had advised all her children to abstain from it. When she was presented with Emma she thought her unsuitable to be the wife of her ambitious and talented son, being neither young enough nor clever enough, and the daughter of poor gentry, in her view the worst possible group from which to choose a bride.

Defying their families, the young couple was married just as Hardy began to establish himself as a novelist. They had high hopes of living a literary life on the pattern of Robert Browning and Elizabeth Barrett, since both of them aspired to be writers; but while Hardy was already on the path to success and would become world famous through his novels, Emma was unable to turn her plans for stories into anything publishable. Over the years she gave a great deal of help to her husband, copying out his manuscripts, researching for him, and on at least one occasion making a suggestion for a scene in a novel, *Tess of the D'Urbervilles*, in which she suggested the incident of the jewels Angel Clare was given for his bride. But although there was a degree of collaboration, essentially Hardy worked on his own. Their paths diverged intellectually, and he retreated further into the world of his imagination. Emma saw and said that he loved the women he imagined far better than any real woman, and Hardy indeed created a gallery of strikingly original and attractive heroines. Not all his loves were fictional; he also fell in love with several real women in the later years of their marriage, all of them with literary ambitions of their own, and drawn to Hardy by his fame. Had there been children, things might have been happier for both Hardys, but there were none.

By the end of the 1890s, they were almost wholly estranged from one another. Emma chose to withdraw from the marital bedroom: "I sleep in an *Attic—or two!*" she wrote to a friend, "Not a sound scarcely penetrates hither. I see the sun, and stars, and moon rise." They no longer took their holidays together, but went their separate ways. In her youth, Emma had shared, or at any rate not minded, his indifference to religion, but as she aged she became pious, and was shocked and upset when he attacked the Church of England in his novel *Jude the Obscure* in 1897. She supported women's rights—as Hardy himself did—and took some interest in public affairs, but she was unworldly and easy to make fun of. As she lost her looks, she dressed oddly, favoring vast, elaborate hats and flowing dresses. Visitors to Max Gate, the house Hardy built for them outside Dorchester, close to his birthplace, were sometimes embarrassed by her inconsequential remarks and her habit of allowing the household cats to sit on the dining table during meals. Worse, Emma took to speaking slightingly about her husband to visitors, and rudely about his work. Hardy could be rude in turn, sending her out of the room over the protests of William Butler Yeats and Henry Newbolt when they came to Max Gate to present him with the Gold Medal of the Royal Society of Literature. Those who disliked Emma suggested that she was mentally deranged, "strange in her head" as her sister-in-law Mary Hardy put it, and after her death Hardy was persuaded that she had suffered from mental problems, especially when he found the journals in which she complained about his behavior. These he subsequently destroyed. Yet she remained perfectly capable of organizing whatever she wanted to do for herself, and when she was seventy she wrote a clear and delicate memoir of her early life. She was by no means the mad woman in the attic, only a slightly scatty English countrywoman, suffering from disappointment and loneliness.

From 1906, Hardy was in love with Florence Dugdale, a young woman who wrote him a fan letter, traveled to Dorset to call on him, flattered him, and sought his advice and help with her own writing, which was undistinguished. He gave her introductions to editors and took her on holiday; she did some secretarial work for him and he helped her to place a few short stories and articles. In due course Florence introduced herself to Emma also, and there was a period of black farce when both Hardys wanted her as their best friend. The situation remained unresolved, with Hardy still attached to Florence, and still married to Emma, in 1912, the year of Emma's death.

Emma remained settled in the attic at Max Gate, looked after by a maid. There she read, wrote, and sewed, and often had her meals brought up from the kitchen to eat alone. She rarely came down to see visitors, but went out into the garden by herself to tend her flowers and to summon the birds she liked to feed, grown so tame they would sit on her arms. If she wanted to visit friends, she would hire a car to fetch her and bring her back. The Hardys did not go out together and hardly spoke to one another.

Her seventy-second birthday went uncelebrated in November, 1912. She had not felt well, and the doctor had seen her, but she had refused to allow him to examine her, and he did not think there was anything seriously wrong. Then, early in the morning of November 27, her maid Dolly went to her as usual and found her alarmingly changed since the night before, and in severe pain. She did not ask for the doctor to be sent for, only for Dolly to fetch her husband. Dolly ran down to Hardy in his study, where he was making an early start on his day's work. He told her to straighten her collar and went up to his wife's bedroom. He spoke her name, "Em, Em—don't you know me?" But she was already unconscious, and within minutes she stopped breathing.

No one could have predicted the effect Emma's death had on Hardy. He immediately began to mourn like a lover. He had her body brought down and placed in the coffin at the foot of his bed, where it remained for three days and nights until the funeral. And he began almost at once to write, revisiting the early love between them in his mind with an intensity that expressed itself in a series of poems. "One forgets all the recent years and differences," he wrote to a friend, "and the mind goes back to the early times when each was much to the other—in her case and mine intensely much." He described himself as being "in flower" as a poet, and he was more productive than he had ever been. He had not forgotten Florence, but his imagination was entirely taken up with Emma, with remorse, and with memories.

The elegies he produced are among the most original ever written, in feeling and in the handling of language and verse forms. They are both conversational and lyrical. Some are desolate, some humorous—one describes her habit when alive of leaving home without bothering to say good-bye, just as she has done in death. They do not spare the truth about the unhappiness suffered by wife and husband, but they move into the past with an expansiveness and panache he had never found before. He speaks to her, he gives her a voice, he conjures her up, sometimes a ghost, sometimes the elderly woman who liked parties and hats and fashion catalogues; more often the girl of long ago, wearing an "air-blue gown," or with her "bright hair flapping free." And he recalls how she seemed to him once a sublime, almost Homeric woman, "Fair-eyed and white shouldered, broad-browed and brown-tressed." He talks to her about her past self, "With your nut-coloured hair, / And gray eyes, and rose-flush coming and going." He remembers how the sunset light over the sea, with its "dipping blaze," colored her young face "fire-red." He relives a moment when he walked with her on a rainy road and they exchanged the words that changed their lives.

At the same time he knows that she is "past love, praise, indifference, blame." She is shut in her grave, "the clodded shell / Of her tiny cell." She is wrapped in her shroud, with the rain that she hates—or hated—beating down on her. She is not there where he expects to see her working in the garden in the evening, and when he returns from his walk the house where she should be is empty of her. He needs to speak to her and to see her, although he knows he cannot. One of the functions of the poetry is that it allows him to. It keeps him balanced between the possible and the impossible, as the bereaved need to be, so that he can sorrow, and then rejoice, and then admit that the rejoicing cannot change how things are.

~

The poems trace a journey that starts with unanswerable questions he puts to himself in "The Going": Why did she go without a goodbye, why does he still see her in his mind, why did they never revisit their early haunts, where "Life unrolled us its very best"? This lyrical start is followed by something entirely different. "Your Last Drive" is colorless, mundane, and modern in reference, to the car and the lights of the borough, and in the plainness of the talk between husband and wife. It draws on an actual November evening when she went out in a hired car alone in the last week of her life. Her words from the grave are unsentimental, even sharp, the voice of the angry wife chiding the husband who neglected her and adding that she does not care. Then suddenly in the last stanza the two words "Dear ghost" change the feeling of the poem to tenderness for a moment, before returning to bleak acceptance of death as final and absolute. Rarely quoted, perhaps because it is not lyrical, this stark poem is among the finest and most surprising.

Two quieter, more conventional verses, "The Walk" and "Rain on a Grave," follow. Then a great lyrical leap occurs in "I Found Her Out There," with its driving rhythm, short lines with only two stresses, all color, light, movement, landscape and seascape, and the young Emma set before us, flapping hair and red cheeks, and "thought-bound brow" as she thinks over the story of the old kingdom of Lyonnesse sunk beneath the waves. There is a brilliant emendation in the fourth line where Hardy coins a compound word to describe the air that blows over the north Cornish cliffs. He first wrote "sharp-edged air," a good image, but then did better, coming up with a conceit worthy of Shakespeare, making it "salt-edged air," the new word catching exactly what you taste and smell as you inhale the air on the cliff top.

"The Haunter" again gives dead Emma a voice, as a ghost replaying old habits. She describes how she used to "Hover and hover a few feet from him," when he did not speak to her or invite her to join him on any journey—whereas now she hovers invisibly and he speaks to her and "wants me with him / More than he used to do." It is honest about the pathos of the living Emma as she tried to be a companionable wife and was repulsed: a very sad poem.

Now comes "The Voice." The first words go straight to the point: "Woman much missed." You might think he had written down what was in his heart immediately, but the manuscript shows that his first draft suggested something more complicated and even sinister: "O woman weird." Second thoughts brought simplicity:

> Woman much missed, how you call to me, call to me,
> Saying that now you are not as you were

> When you had changed from the one who was all to me,
> But as at first, when our day was fair.

The "call to me, call to me" is made into a wail of grief by the "Woman much missed" before them—a line of lamenting dactyls. The woman is trying to reach him and explain what her death means. She is making Hardy look at three different bits of time, the long-ago past when he and Emma had been true lovers, the recent past when they were estranged, and "now," when she tells him she is again as she was in the distant past. (This explains the force of the "woman weird" he began with—she can time-travel inside her grave.)

He goes on to picture her as she used to be, waiting for him to arrive at Launceston railway station. Again, he made a change to the last line, from the dullish "Even to the original hat and gown" to the exquisite "original air-blue gown," that lifts and lights the whole poem, telling us it was summer, and how she stood out luminously in the drab railway station.

> Can it be you that I hear? Let me view you, then,
> Standing as when I drew near to the town
> Where you would wait for me: yes, as I knew you then,
> Even to the original air-blue gown!

Then, to close the poem, he alters the shape and rhythm of the last stanza, reducing the lines as he finds himself reduced, unable to keep his imagination working, brought to his lowest ebb: "Thus I." No air-blue to lift him now, he is merely an old man who can hardly move forward in the north wind among a few skeletal autumn trees, and faltering. In this bleakness the woman's voice is still heard, but with no possibility of an answer or an exchange.

The last seven poems of the series relate to Hardy's visit to Cornwall, where he had not been for forty years. He went in

March, 1913, taking his taciturn brother with him, and leaving Florence in residence at Max Gate. The two men stayed at a hotel in Boscastle, and Hardy arranged for a memorial to Emma to be put up in the church at St Juliot, where she had lived. More important, he walked alone over the remembered paths and clifftops. Out of this came poems bolder and more complex than the earlier ones. "After a Journey" has a rich, subtle, and sustained music through which he conjures up cliff, waters, cave, and waterfall, Emma's gray eyes and nut-colored hair and the "then fair hour in the then fair weather." "Hereto I come to interview a ghost," he began an early draft, in a curiously modern idiom, then changed to "Hereto I come to view a voiceless ghost." You have to read to the last stanza before you understand that he is walking by night, the only time ghosts are allowed to appear:

> Soon you will have, Dear, to vanish from me,
> For the stars close their shutters and the dawn whitens hazily.

His imagination has allowed him to see shape and color as he follows her ghost through the landscape, her gray eyes, her nut-colored hair, the rose-flush coming and going on her cheeks. Having tracked her down, he questions her about "the dark space wherein I have lacked you"—meaning, it seems, the long years of their estrangement. But she gives no answer, or her answer is to lead him silently to the places where they were once happy. Dawn is coming, she will disappear, and he ends by asking her to bring him again to those happy places, telling her he is "just the same" as he was when "our days were a joy, and our paths through flowers." She has said nothing: in this poem she is the "voiceless ghost."

"Beeny Cliff" is an ecstatic hymn to the beauty of the "wandering western sea" and the young Emma riding on the cliff top, "The woman whom I loved so, and who loyally loved me."

It is a love poem and a lament in galloping anapaests, a pure lyric of fifteen lines, flawlessly done. What comes to mind is Hardy's recollection of his father playing the fiddle to which he danced as a small child, in an ecstasy but with tears in his eyes that he tried to hide; surely the germ of his own rhythmical inventiveness and lyric skill was there.

"At Castle Boterel" reverts to the plain telling of the past, "the junction of lane and highway" and the drizzle that "bedrenches the waggonette," prosaically building to the least prosaic claim possible to make—that the single minute in which the lovers declared their feeling for one another is preserved forever in the rocks beside the road:

> . . . was there ever
> A time of such quality, since or before,
> In that hill's story? To one mind never . . .

The poem ends with the image of the old Hardy watching the scene through the present rain, the past getting smaller and smaller, the image of sand in the hour-glass for his life running out, and the last image of the traveler and the country he has passed through and now will not revisit:

> I look and see it there, shrinking, shrinking,
> I look back at it amid the rain
> For the very last time; for my sand is sinking,
> And I shall traverse old love's domain
> Never again.

The distinguished English critic Barbara Hardy (no relation) has written well of how "Hardy uses his poetry in ways that require the reader to experience checks, halts, gaps, limited access and impassable thresholds," but while this is true of much of his work, what makes his elegies unusual is that they are direct, even confessional, and do not leave the reader groping to follow or understand what he has to say about death and its effect on the living. His intention was not to write consolatory verse, simply to report on his own experience, but the poems resonate for many readers because they are so open.

The last poem in the sequence, as he originally published it, is one of the boldest. He chose an odd and difficult metrical structure, nine-line stanzas with a long first and last line and seven very short lines sandwiched between. He starts awkwardly, with an unnamed "I" observing "a man I know" who is old, half mad and obsessed with something he can see as he looks out over the ocean. Only in the last stanza does he answer the question asked at the end of the first, "What does he see?" The answer brings the poem to a magical conclusion:

> A ghost-girl-rider. And though, toil-tried,
> > He withers daily,
> > Time touches her not,
> > But still she rides gaily
> > In his rapt thought
> > On that shagged and shaly
> > Atlantic spot,
> > And as when first eyed
> Draws rein and sings to the swing of the tide.

The "ghost-girl-rider" and "toil-tried" give a spring to the rhythm, so that the short lines canter away after them like the girl on her horse—and like time that has run away with their happiness, and with her life. Only the poem allows her to pause. This is Hardy's magic. He makes her draw rein, she sings, she is there again, and now that he has written the poem, she is there for as long as the poem is there—a good long time, I would guess.

In addition to the elegies, Hardy wrote many more poems about Emma after her death. Many go back to the time of their first meeting and wooing, a few to the early years of their marriage, others to the unhappy later years. Emma's ghost speaks in one. Several contrast his memories of the time she was alive with other days and experiences after her death. Some record his grief and one, the terrifying "Penance," expresses his remorse at having turned away from her. Three in particular allude to happy years soon after their marriage, at Swanage, and at Sturminster Newton, where they first lived in their own house above the river Stour. One of these, "A Two-Years' Idyll," speaks of how little they valued their happiness at the time, as they looked forward eagerly to new scenes in London, where they soon moved, full of hope and ambition. There is a fragment of a first draft that lays even greater emphasis on how happy they were, beginning, "Never such joy was." In Sturminster, Hardy wrote his most poetic novel, *The Return of the Native*, Emma still believed she might publish her stories, and both hoped there would be children. Life pursued its course differently, and sadly; but it is worth reminding ourselves that there was joy for a time for both of them.

CLAIRE TOMALIN

PHOTOGRAPHS AND ILLUSTRATIONS

The church at St. Juliot, near Boscastle, where Thomas Hardy and Emma Gifford first met and fell in love.

WATERCOLOR, COURTESY OF THE ARTIST, GEORGE WICKHAM.

*Beeny Cliff, located on the north coast of Cornwall,
where Thomas Hardy and Emma Gifford walked
together in 1870, and which Hardy revisited in 1913.*
WATERCOLOR, COURTESY OF THE ARTIST, GEORGE WICKHAM.

Emma Gifford near the
time of her marriage to Hardy.
DORSET COUNTY MUSEUM

Hardy from the time of his marriage in 1874. He had published four novels during the four years of his courtship, and he was making significant money.
DORSET COUNTY MUSEUM

Max Gate, located outside Dorchester, on the south coast of England. Hardy designed the house, and had it built by his brother. In June, 1885, he and Emma moved in. Although each had reservations about the house and the town, they lived out their lives there.

DORSET COUNTY MUSEUM

Hardy with his bicycle at Max Gate. DORSET COUNTY MUSEUM

Emma Hardy in her later years. DORSET COUNTY MUSEUM

Hardy in 1924. DORSET COUNTY MUSEUM

POEMS OF 1912–13

Veteris vestigia flammae

　　—Virgil, *The Aeneid*, Book IV, line 23

THE GOING

Why did you give no hint that night
That quickly after the morrow's dawn,
And calmly, as if indifferent quite,
You would close your term here, up and be gone
      Where I could not follow
      With wing of swallow
To gain one glimpse of you ever anon!

      Never to bid good-bye,
      Or lip me the softest call,
Or utter a wish for a word, while I
Saw morning harden upon the wall,
      Unmoved, unknowing
      That your great going
Had place that moment, and altered all.

Why do you make me leave the house
And think for a breath it is you I see
At the end of the alley of bending boughs
Where so often at dusk you used to be;
      Till in darkening dankness
      The yawning blankness
Of the perspective sickens me!

      You were she who abode
      By those red-veined rocks far West,
You were the swan-necked one who rode
Along the beetling Beeny Crest,
      And, reining nigh me,
      Would muse and eye me,
While Life unrolled us its very best.

Why, then, latterly did we not speak,
Did we not think of those days long dead,
And ere your vanishing strive to seek
That time's renewal? We might have said,
      'In this bright spring weather
      We'll visit together
Those places that once we visited.'

      Well, well! All's past amend,
      Unchangeable. It must go.
I seem but a dead man held on end
To sink down soon.... O you could not know
      That such swift fleeing
      No soul foreseeing—
Not even I—would undo me so!

December 1912

YOUR LAST DRIVE

Here by the moorway you returned,
And saw the borough lights ahead
That lit your face—all undiscerned
To be in a week the face of the dead,
And you told of the charm of that haloed view
That never again would beam on you.

And on your left you passed the spot
Where eight days later you were to lie,
And be spoken of as one who was not;
Beholding it with a heedless eye
As alien from you, though under its tree
You soon would halt everlastingly.

I drove not with you. . . . Yet had I sat
At your side that eve I should not have seen
That the countenance I was glancing at
Had a last-time look in the flickering sheen,
Nor have read the writing upon your face,
'I go hence soon to my resting-place;

'You may miss me then. But I shall not know
How many times you visit me there,
Or what your thoughts are, or if you go
There never at all. And I shall not care.
Should you censure me I shall take no heed,
And even your praises no more shall need.'

True: never you'll know. And you will not mind.
But shall I then slight you because of such?
Dear ghost, in the past did you ever find
The thought 'What profit,' move me much?
Yet abides the fact, indeed, the same,—
You are past love, praise, indifference, blame.

December 1912

THE WALK

You did not walk with me
Of late to the hill-top tree
     By the gated ways,
     As in earlier days;
     You were weak and lame,
     So you never came,
And I went alone, and I did not mind,
Not thinking of you as left behind.

I walked up there to-day
Just in the former way;
     Surveyed around
     The familiar ground
     By myself again:
     What difference, then?
Only that underlying sense
Of the look of a room on returning thence.

RAIN ON A GRAVE

CLOUDS spout upon her
    Their waters amain
    In ruthless disdain,—
Her who but lately
    Had shivered with pain
As at touch of dishonour
If there had lit on her
So coldly, so straightly
    Such arrows of rain:

One who to shelter
    Her delicate head
Would quicken and quicken
    Each tentative tread
If drops chanced to pelt her
    That summertime spills
    In dust-paven rills
When thunder-clouds thicken
    And birds close their bills.

Would that I lay there
    And she were housed here!
Or better, together
Were folded away there
Exposed to one weather
We both,—who would stray there
When sunny the day there,
    Or evening was clear
    At the prime of the year.

Soon will be growing
    Green blades from her mound,
And daisies be showing
    Like stars on the ground,
Till she form part of them—
Ay—the sweet heart of them,
Loved beyond measure
With a child's pleasure
    All her life's round.

31 January 1913

I FOUND HER OUT THERE

I FOUND her out there
On a slope few see,
That falls westwardly
To the salt-edged air,
Where the ocean breaks
On the purple strand,
And the hurricane shakes
The solid land.

I brought her here,
And have laid her to rest
In a noiseless nest
No sea beats near.
She will never be stirred
In her loamy cell
By the waves long heard
And loved so well.

So she does not sleep
By those haunted heights
The Atlantic smites
And the blind gales sweep,
Whence she often would gaze
At Dundagel's famed head,
While the dipping blaze
Dyed her face fire-red;

And would sigh at the tale
Of sunk Lyonnesse,
As a wind-tugged tress
Flapped her cheek like a flail;
Or listen at whiles
With a thought-bound brow
To the murmuring miles
She is far from now.

Yet her shade, maybe,
Will creep underground
Till it catch the sound
Of that western sea
As it swells and sobs
Where she once domiciled,
And joy in its throbs
With the heart of a child.

WITHOUT CEREMONY

It was your way, my dear,
To vanish without a word
When callers, friends, or kin
Had left, and I hastened in
To rejoin you, as I inferred.

And when you'd a mind to career
Off anywhere—say to town—
You were all on a sudden gone
Before I had thought thereon,
Or noticed your trunks were down.

So, now that you disappear
For ever in that swift style,
Your meaning seems to me
Just as it used to be:
'Good-bye is not worth while!

LAMENT

How she would have loved
A party to-day!—
Bright-hatted and gloved,
With table and tray
And chairs on the lawn
Her smiles would have shone
With welcomings. . . .   But
She is shut, she is shut
      From friendship's spell
      In the jailing shell
      Of her tiny cell.

Or she would have reigned
At a dinner to-night
With ardours unfeigned,
And a generous delight;
All in her abode
She'd have freely bestowed
On her guests. . . .   But alas,
She is shut under grass
      Where no cups flow,
      Powerless to know
      That it might be so.

And she would have sought
With a child's eager glance
The shy snowdrops brought
By the new year's advance,
And peered in the rime
Of Candlemas-time
For crocuses . . . chanced

It that she were not tranced
     From sights she loved best;
     Wholly possessed
     By an infinite rest!

And we are here staying
Amid these stale things,
Who care not for gaying,
And those junketings
That used so to joy her,
And never to cloy her
As us they cloy! . . . But
She is shut, she is shut
     From the cheer of them, dead
     To all done and said
     In her yew-arched bed

THE HAUNTER

He does not think that I haunt here nightly:
    How shall I let him know
That whither his fancy sets him wandering
    I, too, alertly go?—
Hover and hover a few feet from him
    Just as I used to do,
But cannot answer the words he lifts me—
    Only listen thereto!

When I could answer he did not say them:
    When I could let him know
How I would like to join in his journeys
    Seldom he wished to go.
Now that he goes and wants me with him
    More than he used to do,
Never he sees my faithful phantom
    Though he speaks thereto.

Yes, I companion him to places
    Only dreamers know,
Where the shy hares print long paces,
    Where the night rooks go;
Into old aisles where the past is all to him,
    Close as his shade can do,
Always lacking the power to call to him,
    Near as I reach thereto!

What a good haunter I am, O tell him!
    Quickly make him know
If he but sigh since my loss befell him
    Straight to his side I go.
Tell him a faithful one is doing
    All that love can do
Still that his path may be worth pursuing,
    And to bring peace thereto.

THE VOICE

WOMAN much missed, how you call to me, call to me,
Saying that now you are not as you were
When you had changed from the one who was all to me,
But as at first, when our day was fair.

Can it be you that I hear? Let me view you, then,
Standing as when I drew near to the town
Where you would wait for me: yes, as I knew you then,
Even to the original air-blue gown!

Or is it only the breeze, in its listlessness
Travelling across the wet mead to me here,
You being ever dissolved to wan wistlessness,
Heard no more again far or near?

    Thus I; faltering forward,
    Leaves around me falling,
Wind oozing thin through the thorn from norward,
    And the woman calling.

December 1912

HIS VISITOR

I COME across from Mellstock while the moon wastes weaker
To behold where I lived with you for twenty years and more:
I shall go in the gray, at the passing of the mail-train,
And need no setting open of the long familiar door
        As before.

The change I notice in my once own quarters!
A formal-fashioned border where the daisies used to be,
The rooms new painted, and the pictures altered,
And other cups and saucers, and no cosy nook for tea
        As with me.

I discern the dim faces of the sleep-wrapt servants;
They are not those who tended me through feeble hours and
    strong,
But strangers quite, who never knew my rule here,
Who never saw me painting, never heard my softling song
        Float along.

So I don't want to linger in this re-decked dwelling,
I feel too uneasy at the contrasts I behold,
And I make again for Mellstock to return here never,
And rejoin the roomy silence, and the mute and manifold
        Souls of old.

1913

A CIRCULAR

As 'legal representative'
I read a missive not my own,
On new designs the senders give
    For clothes, in tints as shown.

Here figure blouses, gowns for tea,
And presentation-trains of state,
Charming ball-dresses, millinery,
    Warranted up to date.

And this gay-pictured, spring-time shout
Of Fashion, hails what lady proud?
Her who before last year ebbed out
    Was costumed in a shroud.

A DREAM OR NO

WHY go to Saint-Juliot? What's Juliot to me?
      Some strange necromancy
      But charmed me to fancy
That much of my life claims the spot as its key.

Yes. I have had dreams of that place in the West,
      And a maiden abiding
      Thereat as in hiding;
Fair-eyed and white-shouldered, broad-browed and brown-tressed.

And of how, coastward bound on a night long ago,
      There lonely I found her,
      The sea-birds around her,
And other than nigh things uncaring to know.

So sweet her life there (in my thought has it seemed)
      That quickly she drew me
      To take her unto me,
And lodge her long years with me. Such have I dreamed.

But nought of that maid from Saint Juliot I see;
      Can she ever have been here,
      And shed her life's sheen here,
The woman I thought a long housemate with me?

Does there even a place like Saint-Juliot exist?
      Or a Vallency Valley
      With stream and leafed alley,
Or Beeny, or Bos with its flounce flinging mist?

February 1913

AFTER A JOURNEY

Hereto I come to view a voiceless ghost;
    Whither, O whither will its whim now draw me?
Up the cliff, down, till I'm lonely, lost,
    And the unseen waters' ejaculations awe me.
Where you will next be there's no knowing,
    Facing round about me everywhere,
      With your nut-coloured hair,
And gray eyes, and rose-flush coming and going.

Yes: I have re-entered your olden haunts at last;
    Through the years, through the dead scenes I have tracked you;
What have you now found to say of our past—
    Scanned across the dark space wherein I have lacked you?
Summer gave us sweets, but autumn wrought division?
    Things were not lastly as firstly well
      With us twain, you tell?
But all's closed now, despite Time's derision.

I see what you are doing: you are leading me on
    To the spots we knew when we haunted here together,
The waterfall, above which the mist-bow shone
    At the then fair hour in the then fair weather,
And the cave just under, with a voice still so hollow
    That it seems to call out to me from forty years ago,
      When you were all aglow,
And not the thin ghost that I now frailly follow!

Ignorant of what there is flitting here to see,
　　The waked birds preen and the seals flop lazily;
Soon you will have, Dear, to vanish from me,
　　For the stars close their shutters and the dawn whitens hazily.
Trust me, I mind not, though Life lours,
　　The bringing me here; nay, bring me here again!
　　　I am just the same as when
Our days were a joy, and our paths through flowers.

Pentargan Bay

A DEATH-DAY RECALLED

BEENY did not quiver,
  Juliot grew not gray,
Thin Vallency's river
  Held its wonted way.
Bos seemed not to utter
  Dimmest note of dirge,
Targan mouth a mutter
  To its creamy surge.

Yet though these, unheeding,
  Listless, passed the hour
Of her spirit's speeding,
  She had, in her flower,
Sought and loved the places—
  Much and often pined
For their lonely faces
  When in towns confined.

Why did not Vallency
  In his purl deplore
One whose haunts were whence he
  Drew his limpid store?
Why did Bos not thunder,
  Targan apprehend
Body and Breath were sunder
  Of their former friend?

BEENY CLIFF

March 1870–March 1913

I

O THE opal and the sapphire of that wandering western sea,
And the woman riding high above with bright hair flapping free—
The woman whom I loved so, and who loyally loved me.

II

The pale mews plained below us, and the waves seemed far away
In a nether sky, engrossed in saying their ceaseless babbling say,
As we laughed light-heartedly aloft on that clear-sunned March day.

III

A little cloud then cloaked us, and there flew an irised rain,
And the Atlantic dyed its levels with a dull misfeatured stain,
And then the sun burst out again, and purples prinked the main.

IV

—Still in all its chasmal beauty bulks old Beeny to the sky,
And shall she and I not go there once again now March is nigh,
And the sweet things said in that March say anew there by and by?

V

What if still in chasmal beauty looms that wild weird western shore,
The woman now is—elsewhere—whom the ambling pony bore,
And nor knows nor cares for Beeny, and will laugh there
    nevermore.

AT CASTLE BOTEREL

As I drive to the junction of lane and highway,
    And the drizzle bedrenches the waggonette,
I look behind at the fading byway,
    And see on its slope, now glistening wet,
        Distinctly yet

Myself and a girlish form benighted
    In dry March weather. We climb the road
Beside a chaise. We had just alighted
    To ease the sturdy pony's load
        When he sighed and slowed.

What we did as we climbed, and what we talked of
    Matters not much, nor to what it led,—
Something that life will not be balked of
    Without rude reason till hope is dead,
        And feeling fled.

It filled but a minute. But was there ever
    A time of such quality, since or before,
In that hill's story? To one mind never,
    Though it has been climbed, foot-swift, foot-sore,
        By thousands more.

Primaeval rocks form the road's steep border,
    And much have they faced there, first and last,
Of the transitory in Earth's long order;
    But what they record in colour and cast
        Is—that we two passed.

And to me, though Time's unflinching rigour,
 In mindless rote, has ruled from sight
The substance now, one phantom figure
 Remains on the slope, as when that night
  Saw us alight.

I look and see it there, shrinking, shrinking,
 I look back at it amid the rain
For the very last time; for my sand is sinking,
 And I shall traverse old love's domain
  Never again.

March 1913

PLACES

NOBODY says: Ah, that is the place
Where chanced, in the hollow of years ago,
What none of the Three Towns cared to know—
The birth of a little girl of grace—
The sweetest the house saw, first or last;
　　　Yet it was so
　　　On that day long past.

Nobody thinks: There, there she lay
In a room by the Hoe, like the bud of a flower,
And listened, just after the bedtime hour,
To the stammering chimes that used to play
The quaint Old Hundred-and-Thirteenth tune
　　　In Saint Andrew's tower
　　　Night, morn, and noon.

Nobody calls to mind that here
Upon Boterel Hill, where the waggoners skid,
With cheeks whose airy flush outbid
Fresh fruit in bloom, and free of fear,
She cantered down, as if she must fall
　　　(Though she never did),
　　　To the charm of all.

Nay: one there is to whom these things,
That nobody else's mind calls back,
Have a savour that scenes in being lack,
And a presence more than the actual brings;
To whom to-day is beneaped and stale,
        And its urgent clack
        But a vapid tale.

Plymouth, March 1913

THE PHANTOM HORSEWOMAN

I

QUEER are the ways of a man I know:
   He comes and stands
   In a careworn craze,
   And looks at the sands
   And the seaward haze
   With moveless hands
   And face and gaze,
   Then turns to go . . .
And what does he see when he gazes so?

II

They say he sees as an instant thing
   More clear than to-day,
   A sweet soft scene
   That was once in play
   By that briny green;
   Yes, notes alway
   Warm, real, and keen,
   What his back years bring—
A phantom of his own figuring.

III

Of this vision of his they might say more:
        Not only there
        Does he see this sight,
        But everywhere
        in his brain—day, night,
        As if on the air
        It were drawn rose-bright—
        Yea, far from that shore
Does he carry this vision of heretofore:

IV

A ghost-girl-rider. And though, toil-tried,
        He withers daily,
        Time touches her not,
        But she still rides gaily
        In his rapt thought
        On that shagged and shaly
        Atlantic spot,
        And as when first eyed
Draws rein and sings to the swing of the tide.

1913

EDITOR'S NOTE

The three poems that follow were not included
by Hardy among the "Poems of 1912–1913"
in the first edition of *Satires of Circumstance*,
but added by him to the second edition.

C.T.

THE SPELL OF THE ROSE

'I MEAN to build a hall anon,
　　　And shape two turrets there,
　　　And a broad newelled stair,
And a cool well for crystal water;
　　　Yes; I will build a hall anon,
　　　Plant roses love shall feed upon,
　　　　And apple-trees and pear.'

He set to build the manor-hall,
　　　And shaped the turrets there,
　　　And the broad newelled stair,
And the cool well for crystal water;
　　　He built for me that manor-hall,
　　　And planted many trees withal,
　　　　But no rose anywhere.

And as he planted never a rose
　　　That bears the flower of love,
　　　Though other flowers throve
Some heart-bane moved our souls to sever
　　　Since he had planted never a rose;
　　　And misconceits raised horrid shows,
　　　　And agonies came thereof.

I'll mend these miseries,' then said I,
　　　And so, at dead of night,
　　　I went and, screened from sight,
That nought should keep our souls in severance,
　　　I set a rose-bush. 'This,' said I,
　　　'May end divisions dire and wry,
　　　　And long-drawn days of blight.'

But I was called from earth—yea, called
    Before my rose-bush grew;
    And would that now I knew
What feels he of the tree I planted,
    And whether, after I was called
    To be a ghost, he, as of old,
      Gave me his heart anew!

Perhaps now blooms that queen of trees
    I set but saw not grow,
    And he, beside its glow—
Eyes couched of the mis-vison that blurred me—
    Ay, there beside that queen of trees
    He sees me as I was, though sees
      Too late to tell me so!

ST. LAUNCE'S REVISITED

SLIP back, Time!
Yet again I am nearing
Castle and keep, uprearing
    Gray, as in my prime.

    At the inn
Smiling nigh, why is it
Not as on my visit
    When hope and I were twin?

    Groom and jade
Whom I found here, moulder;
Strange the tavern-holder,
    Strange the tap-maid.

    Here I hired
Horse and man for bearing
Me on my wayfaring
    To the door desired.

    Evening gloomed
As I journeyed forward
To the faces shoreward,
    Till their dwelling loomed.

    If again
Towards the Atlantic sea there
I should speed, they'd be there
    Surely now as then?...

Why waste thought,
When I know them vanished
Under earth; yea, banished
Ever into nought!

WHERE THE PICNIC WAS

WHERE we made the fire
In the summer time
Of branch and briar
On the hill to the sea,
I slowly climb
Through winter mire,
And scan and trace
The forsaken place
Quite readily.

Now a cold wind blows,
And the grass is gray,
But the spot still shows
As a burnt circle—aye,
And stick-ends, charred,
Still strew the sward
Whereon I stand,
Last relic of the band
Who came that day!

Yes, I am here
Just as last year,
And the sea breathes brine
From its strange straight line
Up hither, the same
As when we four came.
—But two have wandered far
From this grassy rise
Into urban roar
Where no picnics are,
And one—has shut her eyes
For evermore

OTHER POEMS ABOUT EMMA

'WHENEVER I plunge my arm, like this,
In a basin of water, I never miss
The sweet sharp sense of a fugitive day
Fetched back from its thickening shroud of gray.
      Hence the only prime
      And real love-rhyme
      That I know by heart,
      And that leaves no smart,
Is the purl of a little valley fall
About three spans wide and two spans tall
Over a table of solid rock,
And into a scoop of the self-same block;
The purl of a runlet that never ceases
In stir of kingdoms, in wars, in peaces;
With a hollow boiling voice it speaks
And has spoken since hills were turfless peaks.'

'And why gives this the only prime
Idea to you of a real love-rhyme?
And why does plunging your arm in a bowl
Full of spring water, bring throbs to your soul?'

'Well, under the fall, in a crease of the stone,
Though where precisely none ever has known,
Jammed darkly, nothing to show how prized,
And by now with its smoothness opalized,
      Is a drinking-glass:
      For, down that pass
      My lover and I
      Walked under a sky

Of blue with a leaf-wove awning of green,
In the burn of August, to paint the scene,
And we placed our basket of fruit and wine
By the runlet's rim, where we sat to dine;
And when we had drunk from the glass together,
Arched by the oak-copse from the weather,
I held the vessel to rinse in the fall,
Where it slipped, and sank, and was past recall,
Though we stooped and plumbed the little abyss
With long bared arms. There the glass still is.
And, as said, if I thrust my arm below
Cold water in basin or bowl, a throe
From the past awakens a sense of that time,
And the glass we used, and the cascade's rhyme.
The basin seems a pool, and its edge
The hard smooth face of the brook-side ledge,
And the leafy pattern of china-ware
The hanging plants that were bathing there.

'By night, by day, when it shines or lours,
There lies intact that chalice of ours,
And its presence adds to the rhyme of love
Persistently sung by the fall above.
No lip has touched it since his and mine
In turns therefrom sipped lovers' wine.'

SHE OPENED THE DOOR

SHE opened the door of the West to me,
     With its loud sea-lashings,
     And cliff-side clashings
Of waters rife with revelry.

She opened the door of Romance to me,
     The door from a cell
     I had known too well,
Too long, till then, and was fain to flee.

She opened the door of a Love to me,
     That passed the wry
     World-welters by
As far as the arching blue the lea.

She opens the door of the Past to me,
     Its magic lights,
     Its heavenly heights,
When forward little is to see!

1913

WHEN I SET OUT FOR LYONNESSE

(1870)

WHEN I set out for Lyonnesse,
    A hundred miles away,
    The rime was on the spray,
And starlight lit my lonesomeness
When I set out for Lyonnesse
    A hundred miles away.

What would bechance at Lyonnesse
    While I should sojourn there
    No prophet durst declare,
Nor did the wisest wizard guess
What would bechance at Lyonnesse
    While I should sojourn there.

When I came back from Lyonnesse
    With magic in my eyes,
    All marked with mute surmise
My radiance rare and fathomless,
When I came back from Lyonnesse
    With magic in my eyes!

AT THE WORD 'FAREWELL'

SHE looked like a bird from a cloud
    On the clammy lawn,
Moving alone, bare-browed
    In the dim of dawn.
The candles alight in the room
    For my parting meal
Made all things withoutdoors loom
    Strange, ghostly, unreal.

The hour itself was a ghost,
    And it seemed to me then
As of chances the chance furthermost
    I should see her again.
I beheld not where all was so fleet
    That a Plan of the past
Which had ruled us from birthtime to meet
    Was in working at last:

No prelude did I there perceive
    To a drama at all,
Or foreshadow what fortune might weave
    From beginnings so small;
But I rose as if quicked by a spur
    I was bound to obey,
And stepped through the casement to her
    Still alone in the gray.

'I am leaving you. . . . Farewell!' I said,
    As I followed her on
By an alley bare boughs overspread;
    'I soon must be gone!'
Even then the scale might have been turned
        Against love by a feather,
—But crimson one cheek of hers burned
        When we came in together.

ON A DISCOVERED CURL OF HAIR

When your soft welcomings were said,
This curl was waving on your head,
And when we walked where breakers dinned
It sported in the sun and wind,
And when I had won your words of grace
It brushed and clung about my face.
Then, to abate the misery
Of absentness, you gave it to me.

Where are its fellows now? Ah, they
For brightest brown have donned a gray,
And gone into a caverned ark,
Ever unopened, always dark!

Yet this one curl, untouched of time,
Beams with live brown as in its prime,
So that it seems I even could now
Restore it to the living brow
By bearing down the western road
Till I had reached your old abode.

February 1913

THE TRESSES

'WHEN the air was damp
It made my curls hang slack
As they kissed my neck and back
While I footed the salt-aired track
    I loved to tramp.

'When it was dry
They would roll up crisp and tight
As I went on in the light
Of the sun, which my own sprite
    Seemed to outvie.

'Now I am old;
And have not one gay curl
As I had when a girl
For dampness to unfurl
    Or sun uphold!'

IF YOU HAD KNOWN

       If you had known
When listening with her to the far-down moan
Of the white-selvaged and empurpled sea,
And rain came on that did not hinder talk,
Or damp your flashing facile gaiety
In turning home, despite the slow wet walk
By crooked ways, and over stiles of stone;
       If you had known

       You would lay roses,
Fifty years thence, on her monument, that discloses
Its graying shape upon the luxuriant green;
Fifty years thence to an hour, by chance led there.
What might have moved you?—yea, had you foreseen
That on the tomb of the selfsame one, gone where
The dawn of every day is as the close is,
       You would lay roses!

1920

TWO LIPS

I KISSED them in fancy as I came
    Away in the morning glow:
I kissed them through the glass of her picture-frame:
    She did not know.

I kissed them in love, in troth, in laughter,
    When she knew all; long so!
That I should kiss them in a shroud thereafter
    She did not know.

THE LAST PERFORMANCE

'I AM playing my oldest tunes,' declared she,
    'All the old tunes I know,—
Those I learnt ever so long ago.'
—Why she should think just then she'd play them
    Silence cloaks like snow.

When I returned from the town at nightfall
    Notes continued to pour
As when I had left two hours before:
'It's the very last time,' she said in closing;
    'From now I play no more.'

A few morns onward found her fading,
    And, as her life outflew,
I thought of her playing her tunes right through;
And I felt she had known of what was coming,
    And wondered how she knew.

1912

PENANCE

'WHY do you sit, O pale thin man,
    At the end of the room
By that harpsichord, built on the quaint old plan?
    —It is cold as a tomb,
And there's not a spark within the grate;
    And the jingling wires
    Are as vain desires
    That have lagged too late.'

'Why do I? Alas, far times ago
    A woman lyred here
In the evenfall; one who fain did so
    From year to year;
And, in loneliness bending wistfully,
    Would wake each note
    In sick sad rote,
    None to listen or see!

'I would not join. I would not stay,
    But drew away,
Though the winter fire beamed brightly…. Aye!
    I do to-day
What I would not then; and the chill old keys,
    Like a skull's brown teeth
    Loose in their sheath,
    Freeze my touch; yes, freeze.'

THE PROSPECT

THE twigs of the birch imprint the December sky
    Like branching veins upon a thin old hand;
I think of summer-time, yes, of last July,
      When she was beneath them, greeting a gathered band
        Of the urban and bland.

Iced airs wheeze through the skeletoned hedge from the north,
    With steady snores, and a numbing that threatens snow,
And skaters pass; and merry boys go forth
      To look for slides. But well, well do I know
        Whither I would go!

December 1912

SOMETHING TAPPED

SOMETHING tapped on the pane of my room
    When there was never a trace
Of wind or rain, and I saw in the gloom
    My weary Belovéd's face.

'O I am tired of waiting,' she said,
    'Night, morn, noon, afternoon;
So cold it is in my lonely bed,
    And I thought you would join me soon!'

I rose and neared the window-glass,
    But vanished thence had she:
Only a pallid moth, alas,
    Tapped at the pane for me.

August 1913

Do YOU recall
That day in Fall
When we walked towards Saint Alban's Head,
On thistledown that summer had shed,
Or must I remind you?
Winged thistle-seeds which hitherto
Had lain as none were there, or few,
But rose at the brush of your petticoat-seam
(As ghosts might rise of the recent dead),
And sailed on the breeze in a nebulous stream
Like a comet's tail behind you:
You don't recall
That day in Fall?

Then do you remember
That sad November
When you left me never to see me more,
And looked quite other than theretofore,
As if it could not *be* you?
And lay by the window whence you had gazed
So many times when blamed or praised,
Morning or noon, through years and years,
Accepting the gifts that Fortune bore,
Sharing, enduring, joys, hopes, fears!
Well: I never more did see you.—
Say you remember
That sad November!

HE PREFERS HER EARTHLY

THIS after-sunset is a sight for seeing,
Cliff-heads of craggy cloud surrounding it.
    —And dwell you in that glory-show?
You may; for there are strange strange things in being,
        Stranger than I know.

Yet if that chasm of splendour claim your presence
Which glows between the ash cloud and the dun,
    How changed must be your mortal mould!
Changed to a firmament-riding earthless essence
        From what you were of old:

All too unlike the fond and fragile creature
Then known to me. . . . Well, shall I say it plain?
    I would not have you thus and there,
But still would grieve on, missing you, still feature
        You as the one you were.

AN UPBRAIDING

Now I am dead you sing to me
    The songs we used to know,
But while I lived you had no wish
    Or care for doing so.

Now I am dead you come to me
    In the moonlight, comfortless;
Ah, what would I have given alive
    To win such tenderness!

When you are dead, and stand to me
    Not differenced, as now,
But like again, will you be cold
    As when we lived, or how?

LOOKING AT A PICTURE
ON AN ANNIVERSARY

But don't you know it, my dear,
    Don't you know it,
That this day of the year
(What rainbow-rays embow it!)
We met, strangers confessed,
    But parted—blest?

Though at this query, my dear,
    There in your frame
Unmoved you still appear,
You must be thinking the same,
But keep that look demure
    Just to allure.

And now at length a trace
    I surely vision
Upon that wistful face
Of old-time recognition,
Smiling forth, 'Yes, as you say,
    It is the day.'

For this one phase of you
    Now left on earth
This great date must endue
With pulsings of rebirth?—
I see them vitalize
    Those two deep eyes!

But if this face I con
　　Does not declare
Consciousness living on
Still in it, little I care
To live myself, my dear,
　　Lone-labouring here!

Spring 1913

THE SHADOW ON THE STONE

I WENT by the Druid stone
That broods in the garden white and lone,
And I stopped and looked at the shifting shadows
That at some moments fall thereon
From the tree hard by with a rhythmic swing,
And they shaped in my imagining
To the shade that a well-known head and shoulders
Threw there when she was gardening.

I thought her behind my back,
Yea, her I long had learned to lack,
And I said: 'I am sure you are standing behind me,
Though how do you get into this old track?'
And there was no sound but the fall of a leaf
As a sad response; and to keep down grief
I would not turn my head to discover
That there was nothing in my belief.

Yet I wanted to look and see
That nobody stood at the back of me;
But I thought once more: 'Nay, I'll not unvision
A shape which, somehow, there may be.'
So I went on softly from the glade,
And left her behind me throwing her shade,
As she were indeed an apparition—
My head unturned lest my dream should fade.

Begun 1913: finished 1916

ONCE AT SWANAGE

THE SPRAY sprang up across the cusps of the moon,
    And all its light loomed green
    As a witch-flame's weirdsome sheen
At the minute of an incantation scene;
And it greened our gaze—that night at demilune.

Roaring high and roaring low was the sea
    Behind the headland shores:
    It symboled the slamming of doors,
Or a regiment hurrying over hollow floors. . . .
And there we two stood, hands clasped; I and she!

THE MUSICAL BOX

LIFELONG to be
Seemed the fair colour of the time;
That there was standing shadowed near
A spirit who sang to the gentle chime
Of the self-struck notes, I did not hear,
    I did not see.

    Thus did it sing
To the mindless lyre that played indoors
As she came to listen for me without:
'O value what the nonce outpours—
This best of life—that shines about
    Your welcoming!'

    I had slowed along
After the torrid hours were done,
Though still the posts and walls and road
Flung back their sense of the hot-faced sun,
And had walked by Stourside Mill, where broad
    Stream-lilies throng.

    And I descried
The dusky house that stood apart,
And her, white-muslined, waiting there
In the porch with high-expectant heart,
While still the thin mechanic air
    Went on inside.

At whiles would flit
Swart bats, whose wings, be-webbed and tanned,
Whirred like the wheels of ancient clocks:
She laughed a hailing as she scanned
Me in the gloom, the tuneful box
　　　Intoning it.

　　　Lifelong to be
I thought it. That there watched hard by
A spirit who sang to the indoor tune,
'O make the most of what is nigh!'
I did not hear in my dull soul-swoon—
　　　I did not see.

Yes; such it was;
Just those two seasons unsought,
Sweeping like summertide wind on our ways;
Moving, as straws,
Hearts quick as ours in those days;
Going like wind, too, and rated as nought
Save as the prelude to plays
Soon to come—larger, life-fraught:
Yes; such it was.

'Nought' it was called,
Even by ourselves—that which springs
Out of the years for all flesh, first or last,
Commonplace, scrawled
Dully on days that go past.
Yet, all the while, it upbore us like wings
Even in hours overcast:
Aye, though this best thing of things,
'Nought' it was called!

What seems it now?
Lost: such beginning was all;
Nothing came after: romance straight forsook
Quickly somehow
Life when we sped from our nook,
Primed for new scenes with designs smart and tall. . . .
—A preface without any book,
A trumpet uplipped, but no call;
That seems it now.

FURTHER READINGS

Pertinent Works by Thomas Hardy

Hardy, Thomas. *The Complete Poems of Thomas Hardy*. James Gibson, ed. New York: Macmillan, 1978.

———. *A Pair of Blue Eyes*. 1873. o.p. Available on line at Project Gutenberg and Google Books. This novel describes the Cornish landscape where Thomas Hardy and Emma Gifford met, and offers parallels to their relationship.

Biographical

Gittings, Robert. *The Young Thomas Hardy*. New York: Penguin, 1978.

———. *The Older Hardy*. New York: Penguin, 1980.

Hardy, Emma. *Some Recollections*. Evelyn Hardy and Robert Gittings, eds. Freeport, New York: Books for Libraries Press, 1972.

———. *Diaries*. Richard H. Taylor, ed. Manchester, England: Carcanet New Press, 1985.

Hardy, Thomas. *The Life and Work of Thomas Hardy*. Michael Millgate, ed. Athens, Georgia: University of Georgia Press, 1985.

Millgate, Michael, ed. *Letters of Emma and Florence Hardy*. New York: Oxford University Press, 1996.

Tomalin, Claire. *Thomas Hardy*. New York: Penguin, 2007.

Criticism

Auden, W. H. "A Literary Transference," *Southern Review*, Thomas Hardy Centennial Issue, Summer, 1940.

Davie, Donald. *Thomas Hardy and British Poetry*. London and Boston: Routledge & Keegan Paul PLC, 1978.

Hardy, Barbara. *Thomas Hardy: Imagining Imagination in Hardy's Poetry and Fiction*. London: Athlone Press, 2000.

Hynes, Samuel. Introduction, *Thomas Hardy: Selected Poetry*. New York: Oxford University Press, 2009.

Larkin, Philip. "A Poet's Teaching for Poets" in *Thomas Hardy, Poems: A Casebook*. James Gibson and Trevor Johnson, eds. New York: Palgrave Macmillan, 1980.

Schwartz, Delmore. "Poetry and Belief in Thomas Hardy," *Southern Review*, Thomas Hardy Centennial Issue, Summer, 1940.